THE

3 C's

The only book you need to find your life partner

*Or how to stop screwing up your personal life
and making everyone around you miserable.*

RONNIE J. PACE

The 3 C's

Published by
Flagstone Books
Austin, Texas

First Edition, February 2013
Second Edition, May 2015

ISBN-13: 978-1482644432
ISBN-10: 1482644436
BISAC: Self-Help / Personal Growth / Happiness

THE 3 C's

Dedication

This book is dedicated to and I am thankful....

For my relationship with God; for by his grace, I was given a second chance at age thirty-two to continue experiencing opportunities for life's enjoyment as well as disappointments; to embrace my faith when all hope has left me; to be a witness to those, who like I was and still am, in need of a kind word, a prayer and a reminder as to why I should be thankful, for the dire as well as the good. Who knew that at the age of sixty-six I would be afforded another opportunity to be in significant need of a kind word, a prayer and a reminder as to why I should be thankful? In March 2013, I was diagnosed with invasive ductal carcinoma; yes, male breast cancer. A mastectomy was performed on my right breast the following month—definitely not on my list of things with which I wanted to deal, but as the axiom goes, "make lemonade from lemons." This is what I have done. At MD Anderson Hospital, I currently serve on The Patient and Family Advisory Council as well as the Steering Committee of MyCancerConnection. I am also working with Volunteer Services to establish a Male Breast Cancer Survivors' Support Team.

For my wife, Judith, for the why and the how I came to find relationship happiness; for the strength to persevere through all that life throws at me; for the good, the bad and the sad. Judy gives me the earthly courage to face each day and stay in the fight; a good wife is truly more valuable than gold and jewels.

For my children and grandchildren, who, by their youth and innocence, give rise to the occasion for me to feel younger than I would have without them. Of course, any decisions that they make that are not in their best interest are obviously made as a result of their not paying attention to my counsel. I say this jokingly, of course. I am bursting with pride for each of them.

For my friends, some of whom, I suspect, are influenced by forces of evil and who attacked me without compassion. To those friends and acquaintances who joined in the attacks or who stood by while I got the stuffing knocked out of me, I still wish you well.

For my real friends who never doubted my honesty and commitment to doing right by all people. I only hope I am as good a friend to you as you are to me.

Contents

Acknowledgments

I would like to thank all those who have helped me write this book, knowingly or otherwise. Thank you for the answers to my seemingly endless questions and probing of your personal relationships and thoughts.

Any chance of your finding your thoughts in this book is as remote as it is possible. I believe it is intrinsic in each of us that we want a supportive and satisfying relationship.

The axiom that only you can make you happy has always been an enigma to me; yet it is true. The right relationship, however, can go a long way in adding to your happiness, if you are first happy with yourself.

For everyone who wants companionship and not just a wet nose, I encourage you not to give up. Perhaps it is like fishing, using the wrong bait, the wrong technique or the wrong fishing spot. Spend some time where you currently are; if it's not working, move on; change yourself if necessary and be confident. If you don't feel confident, pretend until you do; people notice, and it will be beneficial in your quest for relationship happiness. I believe there is a person looking for someone just like you; someone with whom he can spend the rest of his life in harmony and exhilarating excitement.

I feel that way because I, as so many have and are doing, lived through a series of relationship roller coasters. High school romance is as good as any to start learning, and if you were lucky enough to find the person that after the years have passed is still the one that makes you hurry back from a trip, the one that you feel can never be replaced, congratulations, the rest of us weren't that lucky. Most of us can remember the adolescent heartaches; and now, the young and older adult, heartbreaks. We should have learned something, but for many of us, we did not. It's time to stop making the same mistakes and utilize a methodology that will put you in a place that you had only thought was for others; someone to share feelings of excitement, happiness, contentment and dreams that are truly bigger than life and beyond your wildest expectations.

Foreword to the Second Edition
by George Wier

The 3 C's is fundamentally a workbook. It is decidedly "hands-on." That is to say that the reader is expected to *do* something, not just *think* it. I've never seen a "think-your-way" book that ever had any application in the real world. Yes, I'm sure that thoughts are indeed things, and if your thinking isn't right, well, you'll probably miss the mark when it comes to action in the real world. But I'm not one hundred percent sold on that, either. I've found that there is no substitute for getting your hands dirty, whether its fiddling with engines or airplanes, math problems or, in this case, relationships. I'd say that treating this book from the start as something *to do* will help you in the long run. And let me tell you, the run can be long indeed.

Also, Ronnie Pace is definitely a *doing* kind of guy. He regularly traverses the width and breadth of Texas as if it's his own personal back forty. When he wants to meet me for coffee, he takes the drive up from Kerrville—close on to a hundred miles—and seems to think nothing of it.

This brings me back around full circle to *The 3C's*. Ronnie told me he was writing this book several years ago, to which I said, "Uh huh," like I do with everyone who says that. You see, I'm a writer by trade. I write fiction, and I write a lot of it. Writing is in my blood. So when someone says they're writing something, let me tell you, you're talking to someone who writes daily, and has finished more projects that he's got fingers and toes. But when Ronnie said this—and I had known Ronnie for some time, and let me tell you, he's the last person I would have ever expected to write anything other than a contract or, possibly, a check—I took notice. I asked him what it was about. Oh. It was non-fiction. There went a good portion of my immediate interest. Except for one thing. It was Ronnie Pace saying it!

A little something about Ronnie, here. On first meeting, when he shakes your hand, you know your hand has been shaken. He's got an iron grip, he has sharp, intelligent and knowing eyes, and a thin smile that seems to be holding a little something back. Judgment, possibly. I got the feeling on our first meeting that he knew everything there was to know about me before two words were out of my mouth.

And so it goes with this book. In it, he talks to *you*, and it's like he's talking to his best friend. Also—and please believe me—he's actually saying *exactly* what he's saying, and he's doing it without any apology, without any fanfare, and it's dead-on. He means it. Every word.

When Ronnie handed me his manuscript, I settled in one evening as the sun was going down and started reading. Let me tell you, that first night with his manuscript, I didn't stop. When I was done, I called him on the phone, and despite the lateness of the hour, he answered.

There was one thing I impressed upon him that evening. In answer to his question to me as to whether the book would mean something—in the context of what he referred to as a "real writer," meaning, of course, me—I told him in no uncertain terms, "Ronnie, people read my books and for a few hours I hope they are entertained. Your book will change lives."

Thankfully, he took it to heart.

This book will do that. It will change lives. It may change yours. That is, it will if you let it.

As conventional wisdom has it, you only get out of any activity what you put into it. Therefore, if your wish is to walk away from this book with something more than you brought to it, then please prepare to *work* through this book. By which I mean, of course, prepare to work on *yourself*. Or better yet, prepare to work *with* yourself, because *you* are the subject of this book. Don't forget it for a moment, and all will be well.

George Wier
Austin, Texas
May 2015

Introduction

This book is written to offer a relationship methodology and give hope to those who want to have successful long-term life experiences with another individual; to experience levels of excitement and happiness that heretofore have been only a transient passing of wishful thinking.

Many authors have written books about interpersonal relationships. Some authors are willing to share with you their secrets in finding the perfect relationship; few, however, tell us how to keep it once we find it. I submit to you that there are no perfect relationships. There are, however, relationships that are so fulfilling that the imperfections are inconsequential. We are, simply stated, individual people, unique in every way. The task in finding the relationship that works for you is to make those individual and unique gifts work for you, not against you. By following the process discussed in this book, I believe you will come as close as anyone can in having an opportunity to not only find, but also keep the relationship that meets and exceeds your wants and needs.

The methodology for this book has been gleaned from personal experiences and through observations and discussions with many other individuals. Some of these individuals are in the midst of relationship struggles or have simply given up on the notion of having a relationship void of contentious and seemingly endless conflict. Like most lessons, those learned first-hand, touted oftentimes as the most painful, can be the best. Hopefully, by reading this book and applying the information presented, you can skip some of the painful lessons learned by others. Unfortunately, this book is not written in the context that you can save the relationship you are currently in. However, it is my sincere desire that you will at least know by the end of the book the reason(s) why your relationship is in discord, and with that knowledge, an informed decision can be made as to the direction you want the rest of your life to go in a current or future relationship.

Divorce rates continue to rise. The number of couples that remain married for convenience, perceived necessity, the fear of being alone or a myriad of other excuses is immeasurable, due in part that many are in denial. None of us enter into the relationship of marriage with the pre-disposed idea that marriage is not a life-long commitment; yet many of us are divorced, separated, or living through third-party observed motions of a satisfying relationship. In the midst of conflict, don't we ask ourselves, "Surely, this is not the way relationships are supposed to be?" My answer is, unequivocally, "no, not at all!"

Unless many of us are wrong in our beliefs and assumptions, our time on earth is short and not for practice. After my near-death experience, I told myself that I would not take any day for granted. The trouble is that I am human and thus fall short on a daily basis on many fronts. I, like many, have the best of intentions, but tend to be less than successful in the execution of ideas, promises, and commitments. I have squandered months and even years when I should have been thinking about my promise, "every day is a gift from God; take this second chance and do something for others." I was given a second chance. For that, much was expected; yet I fell short of my responsibility and promise. Through this book and workshops where group sessions can be beneficial, I hope to make up for that lost time by reaching those who are struggling in relationships. In my own defense, I too was lost and confused. I still refer to my notes on which this book was written to keep myself aligned with my wife, my friends and my business associates.

No one would start a journey to an unknown destination without adequate preparation; yet we go into marriage oftentimes with the least amount of interpersonal preparation or worse, information that we have not confirmed to be completely accurate. I have written this book to give us a "road map" or in today's vernacular, GPS, to find the person with whom we not only desire, but with whom we can spend the rest of our life and with the knowledge that person also feels the same about you. I suspect you are thinking, "This is too hard to believe." Good news, believe it. However, it only works like any map; i.e., you have to stay on the road that takes you where you want to go. The concept of this personal "road map" began when I met my wife 18 years ago; she was the initial subject upon which this process was formulated and tested. We have been married since December 1992 and don't profess to have the "perfect" marriage; what we do say is that we are both happier with each other each day we are together; happier than either could have wanted or imagined. This is not to say that there have not been some late nights "discussing" unpleasant issues, but we persist. Our spiritual compatibility includes the belief that the scripture (Eph. 4:26-27, 31-32) referencing the idea of not letting the sun go down on one's anger is critical in good relationships as well as conflict resolution. While conflict is usually unpleasant, if both parties establish and observes "Agreed rules of engagement," the conflict can result in no loss of intimacy and the parties' gaining insight into the other's point of view.

Finding the person with whom to share meaningful and satisfying experiences for the rest of your life is based on each of your individual willingness to be honest with yourself and the other person. For this process to truly work, each person also has to be totally honest with himself and you as well. Trust has to be the first stone laid in the building of a relationship. The procedures you are asked to follow in the later chapters mean nothing if you both cannot begin with trust.

Hopefully you are grasping the concept that there is hope to finding relationship happiness and are sufficiently intrigued. Let's start working on your personal road map; for the non-technically challenged, you know, the techno geeks, locate your GPS coordinates.

Chapter One

Why Do Relationships Fail?

Why do relationships fail? There is no single answer to this question, but my answer is that we don't always know why. We are complex beings, whose behavior is driven by heredity and environment. If we knew the answer to why relationships fail, would we continue to make the same or similar bad choices? I don't think so. It is too easy to blame the failure on a host of social shortcomings that can be brought to reason. I do not have the clinical training necessary to dazzle you, so this book is not filled with psychological information about your "inner child" or bad potty training. It is about using the most basic of cognitive skills most of us have to eliminate bad choices in our quest for a satisfying and rewarding life partner (ship). We need to stop deluding ourselves that "we are always right, and that it is the other person's fault". If successful in following the process, one can relegate the word "blame" to never-never land. We first need to look at ourselves, however, with the most honest of assessments.

Relationships can and do fail for many reasons. Sometimes it is as simple as placing unrealistic values on certain aspects of the relationship. A desired result for you reading this book is that it will eliminate the initial cause of relationship failure, the wrong partner. There is nothing wrong with the person or you; you are just wrong for each other in your individual, current emotional state. In addition, when you finish the book, you will find out that many of the things considered important, really aren't. When you are in a truly mutually satisfying relationship, it is amazing that one of the important things that takes place is the loss of "must have, must win" situations.

Sometimes in the best of relationships, power struggles develop; these occur when neither partner is willing to step back and ask, "Why are we arguing about this" or "Is this issue worth this much discord?" It is imperative that one of you remains focused on the core issue. It is important to keep the discussion centered on the facts. Do you know that it is impossible to argue about facts? An example: "one can argue that the room is too hot or too cold, but it is impossible to argue that the temperature (as recorded by a calibrated thermometer for you scientific types) is 76 degrees Fahrenheit." Therefore, direct the conversation toward how you perceive the room temperature as it relates to you, i.e., "I feel hot when the temperature of the room is 76 degrees Fahrenheit." The power struggle between who is right evaporates when opinions are taken out of the discussion. We are individuals and thus have our own opinions. It does no one any good to bludgeon someone over the head to adopt your opinion just to have the satisfaction of saying you're right. Talk about the facts, and one of life's most time consuming and hurtful situations, senseless arguing, is easily resolved. Remember, you cannot argue about the facts, only opinions.

Long-term memory is great unless your partner uses it to tell you every thing you've done wrong since you both met. Gender specific jokes are made about this issue. Don't believe them. Both genders pull "I remember when you..." Once the issue is resolved, it is over. It is not for later use in making a point or clouding a circumstance in which you find yourself. Conflict resolution will be discussed in more detail later in the book.

Another one of our most basic relationship tenets is that we want to be heard, not only by our partner, but also by our children, supervisor, friends, etc. It is my belief that each of us has an instinctive desire to feel that what we have to say is important and has value. When two partners are struggling with an issue, it is sometimes difficult to listen and validate what we are hearing, especially if it is contradictory to our thinking. If we have adequate listening/communication "tools", the process of listening and validating becomes easier and soon becomes part of your interpersonal skill set. Oftentimes a problem is created when the desire to be heard by our partner occurs when both partners are trying to get validation for what is important to him or her at that moment. A common example occurs when the question is asked, "Who is to say what has the greater personal emotional impact, the stay-at-home spouse/partner with the broken dishwasher or the road warrior coming back from dealing with unreasonable clients, co-workers, etc?" The answer is, of course, that they both need to be heard. They need to be heard without interruption or having the value of their own disappointment or crisis discounted. Failed relationships and poor listening coupled with poor communication skills are probably not just a coincidence. Listening is not hearing. The next paragraph gives more insight into rudimentary listening skills.

This first chapter is written to provide some basic concepts of why relationships fail. It is not to teach in-depth listening/ communication skills. Basic listening/communicating techniques are necessary, however, to achieve the goals put forth in the remaining chapters. One such listening/conversation tool is called "mirroring." This is effective in listening and conversing with anyone. When you hear something that you don't understand or sounds threatening or offensive, try to say to that person, "What I heard you say was... is that what you said?" Many times it was not the message the person had intended for you to hear; he either used a poor choice of words or the wrong emphasis via an emotional delivery. By mirroring, you give the person making the remark an opportunity to clarify what he meant to say; and you, the opportunity not to become defensive. Paraphrased, James 1:19, states, "be quick to hear, slow to speak and slow to anger." It is amazing the number of times we say or hear things totally contradictory to the message intended. However, if the person, after clarifying, intended to make a threatening or offensive statement, you would have to choose an appropriate course of action. We do not enjoy being in a state of distress whether it is mental or physical. We have two basic courses of action; return to a state of peace and assess the situation with calm resolve or move ourselves into a defensive posture, ready to "duke it out." Since we are operating in the vein of life-partner relations, let's agree to proceed with the notion that "duking it out" is not an option.

Imagine being chased by a ferocious animal as your partner is trying to tell you something. Do you really care what he is saying? Even if it is helpful, are you going to stop running and listen? This is another reason relationships get off course. Each partner is too concerned with his or her own needs. Our focus on self is such that the other partner's needs are not even visible on the radar screen. Discussions that begin with "you don't listen" or "you don't care what I am going through" usually can be traced to one partner's feeling of being overwhelmed. It occurs usually at the moment the other partner is wanting to tell him something that is unrelated to the issue or is not perceived to be helpful in resolving the crisis of the moment, i.e., the feeling a ferocious animal is about to overcome him. Cues that can help us determine our as well as our partner's state of agitation exist all around us if we look and listen. Remember as kids how we were taught to cross the street? Look and listen, not really complicated but very informative. Do the same with your partner. How are both your mannerisms—relaxed, tense, angry? The only way effective communication can occur is for both parties to exist in the peaceful and rational areas of their consciousness. Only "open" statements allow for a person to respond. Ask, "how are you feeling" not "you don't feel good, do you?" When we ask or make "closed" remarks or questions, we shut down the other person's ability to effectively communicate. Too often we perceive other people's moods by our own set of comparisons—probably not a good idea, unless you are clairvoyant.

Notes, Questions and Conclusions
This is not a test, you cannot fail, so be honest with yourself.

_____

_____

_____

_____

_____

_____

_____

_____

_____

_____

_____

_____

_____

_____

_____

_____

_____

_____

_____

_____

_____

Chapter Two

There is A Plan

A plan does not have to be complicated to work. The best plan is often simple, easy to remember and execute. It does need to be designed and presented in a way that can be understood and executed with a high degree of certainty in producing a successful outcome by all who need it.

Having said that, how about a plan with just three parts? (Okay, how about three parts with the part in the middle having five sections?) That's it—not very complicated or lengthy. The good news, unlike other complicated fix-yourself books, is that this plan only requires adherence to the execution criteria until you reach a "no-go" item. You are not required to follow the plan with dogged determination only to find that the person (it could be you) does not measure up to a level of desire or assurance that is required. In case you blew past it, you, too, are up for review. Each of you going through the process outlined in later chapters has equal responsibility for determining if you want to go forward with the relationship. Scary? Not really. Would you like to end the relationship with a minimum of emotional and financial impact or wait several years and argue about who gets the house, the car, or the cat?

Relationships can be predictable; do not confuse predictability with boring. It is a joy to face each day with a partner who is your best friend and confidant, a spiritual soul mate, is sexually compatible and, best of all, has you as a reflection of what he gives. Never subscribe to the theory that you should give anything less than 100 percent. Your job, your children, and especially your relationship with your partner deserve 100 percent of your effort. How does that work? It is virtually impossible to give away 100 percent of yourself in the right relationship. I hope you understand this concept more completely after reading and applying the tenets contained within this book. Jobs and children use a different set of commitment scorecards, and this book is not written solely for their benefit. However, your job and children will benefit as a result of true relationship happiness coupled with the lack of relationship discord. Think about the effort you have wasted on so-called important issues in the past, which in the end, really meant very little.

If you use the steps outlined in the next chapters and choose a partner based upon the results of those steps, all facets of your relationship with him/her will be described in words that appear unrealistic to those who don't know how happy you really are. To some it may be too much happiness, but not for me. For the rest of my life,

I want total strangers to continue to stop by our table and say, "You look so happy, just married?" Sadly, we all know of couples that have the look of being married too long. The spark and excitement are gone from the relationship. Keep reading; if you are one of those, there is hope. You had it once, and you can have it again.

With the good news there is always the potential for not so good news. What do we do if we are in a struggling relationship now? You have at least two options. One is to put the book down and continue the road you are on, and do nothing. Two, read the book with an open attitude (remember you could be the one who needs a little tuning up). As you read the book, assess yourself and your partner using the steps presented within. Then, suggest to your partner that you do the steps together after he has had the opportunity to read the book. Herein lies the potential for the not so good news. It is possible that you two are not the ones for each other. Life is full of choices. You may stay where you are and do nothing, knowing that until something or someone makes the effort, nothing will change; or work on your individual personal issues and the resultant relationship problems using new techniques; or third, have the discussion about the house, the car and the cat. I truly hope that number one or three is not the choice you make. Change is difficult for some but not impossible. Do not attempt to change the other person or the relationship. As you both work on your own issues, the relationship will change on its own. The relationship may become more difficult at times, but positive change is possible if you are willing to work on yourself as well as the relationship and both parties give up the notion of having it all their way. I do not like the word compromise; for me, it means conceding or giving in. I became a certified mediator in 1994 for basic (commercial) disputes and certified in 2009 for family disputes. In 2014, I became certified for Child Protective Services mediation. In relationships, mediation or finding the "middle ground" can mean the difference between marriage or divorce, happiness or misery. I have developed the strategy for successful settlement which initially rests on two things: 1. Agree on something, even if it nothing more than "what the time is" and 2. One partner has to be willing to "take less" and the other "give more" than they initially wanted. Once those two points have been determined, find out what is really important to each of you and agree at least on those points, the other stuff is just ego. Once you agree on one point, you will be surprised how many other things on which you will agree. To repeat, once you have delineated the unpleasant issues that may have been in your relationship, the opportunity to address each of them exists. Then decide if changes can be made. Remember I wrote earlier, "It is not always the other person's fault." Choices are made every day that we think will make us happy or provide us with what we want. The truth is that courthouses are full of people that feel they made the right choice and still did not get what they wanted or deserved. The truth is, life is not fair. You may choose to stay where you are and make the best of it; that's o.k. At least you have made a decision with the best information you have ever had. The decision to make no decision is in fact, a decision, i.e.; to do nothing.

The proposed plan for relationship happiness does not guide you into becoming a clone of your partner. It is designed to define certain areas that have been proven to be "deal breakers" in your relationship. The plan is also not intended to "change" anyone. Change is good only if it comes through self-analysis and discovering that one is behaving in ways that are not in his best interest. Lasting change results only if we want it for reasons that only we decide. Good examples of this are people who decide to quit smoking or lose weight. Only when they decide that is is time, will they succeed. Doing it for someone else usually is not successful.

We are who we are, products of heredity and environment. Nothing I have read or in discussions with others has led me to the determination as to which of the two factors has dominance. There are some who believe in divine intervention, providence, luck or opportunity as additional factors. I like it simple. We are born with a certain set of genes, and that is all we are going to get. Some of us have designer genes and some have the discount brand. Bummer luck, but remember what I said, life is not fair. But you can improve the odds of being happy in your relationship. Environmental influences are a bit more flexible. For example, we can move out of our surroundings, if possible, to improve our surroundings, be it neighborhoods, schools or work. I developed the plan presented utilizing the two human factors, heredity and environment. You do not need to be a member of Mensa or born in the right social setting to make good decisions using this book. Life is not that complicated. It is my desire that all who read this book will be able to make an informed decision by simply using nonemotional and common sense criteria. Don't forget, this decision results in one of the most important aspects of your life, finding (and keeping) your life-partner.

Notes, Questions and Conclusions

This is not a test, you cannot fail, so be honest with yourself.

_____

_____

_____

_____

_____

_____

_____

_____

_____

_____

_____

_____

_____

_____

_____

_____

_____

_____

_____

_____

Chapter Three

The Plan Begins—An Overview

The moment for which you have been waiting is here, the plan. Let me repeat in case you were nodding off earlier. "I like things simple," and, as promised, the plan has three main components. They are collectively known as "The Three "C's". To make sure you keep reading, you will have to wait for the five subsections contained in the second part until later. The three main parts are:

- Chemistry
- Compatibility
- Consistency

Now is the time you have to begin making decisions. The first decision is paramount for the plan to work. You and the person you are considering to be your life-partner must agree to be totally and brutally honest. This is not permission to tell the other person what it is about them you don't like; rather it is permission to tell the other person candid information about yourself when asked. If trust is already an issue, why is this person even being considered someone with whom you want to spend the rest of your life?

The two of you must not assume anything from this point forward. Irrevocable agreements must be made between the two of you that regardless of what information you share your verbal or visual judgment of the other person's past, future behavior and/or thoughts cannot be part of the dialogue. Removing any trace of auditory and visual cues from your mannerisms is paramount to the successful exchange of personal, confidential and intimate information. For some, it may be difficult to share honest, intimate and non-intimate thoughts with someone, especially with the expectation that the person will not be judgmental. The importance of sharing personal thoughts between two people and the need for trust cannot be overstated. For the process to work, you must have the peace of mind of not only his or her impartial attitude, but also that no information will be shared with anyone. If a breach of this type occurs, it is a deal breaker. Intimacy is built on trust; this is the first test. This process is for both parties; it is designed so that you know everything about the other person. As the process continues, use your "perfect partner" list to see where you both comparatively stack up. What "perfect partner" list? It is the one you prepared before you began looking for Mr./Mrs. Right. Yes you can have a "perfect partner" list, why not? When you go to the grocery store, you have a grocery list;

for Christmas, you have a Christmas list, etc. Are we so insecure about finding our other half that makes us feel whole that we will not write down those things we want? Spiritual wholeness emanates from our relationship with our higher power, and we know when we do not feel complete in a spiritual sense. Yet, we ignore the secular incomplete feelings. Since this is for the rest of your life, what do you want in a life partner? If you could have it just as you want it, put it on the list. When you read the middle sections of the book, you can review your list to expand or delete items. I believe you will be surprised to find that the things you thought were important in the beginning now seem much less significant.

Notes, Questions and Conclusions

This is not a test, you cannot fail, so be honest with yourself.

_____

_____

_____

_____

_____

_____

_____

_____

_____

_____

_____

_____

_____

_____

_____

_____

_____

_____

_____

_____

_____

_____

_____

_____

_____

_____

_____

_____

_____

_____

_____

_____

_____

_____

_____

_____

_____

_____

_____

_____

_____

Ronnie J. Pace

Chapter Four

The First "C"—Chemistry; Where It All Begins And Maybe Should End

Too much emphasis has been placed on looks, clothes, money and status. When you go into a crowded room, it is impossible to tell the pedigree, financial status or anything about the person who, for some reason, has caught your attention. Clothes perhaps? I submit that it is something you cannot determine, but something. Some call it magnetism, electricity. I call it chemistry.

Here is how it starts for those not in a committed relationship and who still believe in monogamy. You work yourself across the room to get a better look at this individual who seems to have promise, at least from a distance. We have all done this. Admit it. Our heart beats a little faster, we rehearse what captivating and witty dialogue we are going to open the conversation with, check our hair, etc. Then the moment is upon us, and in a few short but agonizing moments, you have made contact. Eye, verbal or touch, time to put up or shut up. Here is where we often go wrong. We pretend to be someone we are not. Be yourself. If it works, great. If not, that's also great as well, and you will find out in subsequent chapters why either way is okay.

Let's start with the false signal. The connection is bad, and the chemistry is going south fast. Don't try to salvage it, go on and enjoy the moment for what it is, a moment in your life that will be forgotten along with many others but without a lot of emotional, financial and physical distress. You have the same right, as others, to choose with whom you want to spend time. Courtesy and tact always take precedent. Be polite and excuse yourself if it is just too painful or uncomfortable to continue the dialogue. Oftentimes we give mixed messages. We think we have to be nice, and that's okay as long as the person you are talking with is not picking up mixed signals that indicate you are interested in extending the conversation over dinner or maybe drinks later. Once again, courtesy and tact should prevail as no one wants to be shunned just because his and your chemistry is not compatible. Remember, it could be you the next time. You would not want to find out that you are not the love of someone's life after all; discarded like yesterday's old newspaper. Of course, there is always the obtuse person that can't take a hint no matter how obvious it is. Always take the high road and feel good about yourself when it is over.

How do you know the object of your attention is the potential Mr./Ms. Wonderful or not? You will know if you allow yourself to see beyond the superficial. Drop all pretenses and pre-conceived ideas as to what it takes to give you the feeling of WOW. It is, or it isn't. You can't force it or hope it will come later. When the chemistry is right, it is that (Are you ready for the answer?) simple. Of the multiple numbers of people in the world with whom you could spend your life, why settle? Get what you want; you both deserve it. For now, go on faith. I am telling you that there is someone looking for you right now, and you will both miss out if either settles for less. Okay, as one popular game show host used to say, there was not a love connection. Perk up, that means he/she is still out there and probably looking for you, so why give up? What have you lost, a little time? What is time as compared to a lifetime of loneliness or living in a dysfunctional relationship? The necessity of ending the conversation early is so no one feels compelled to invest physical energy or money in a relationship that is not going anywhere for the long haul. If you only want companionship, that is great; but know that from the onset. If you want one-nighters, knock yourself out, but this book is not for you anyway. The system outlined in the book works. But like all successful plans, it only works if the plan parameters are followed. These parameters are designed for long term relationships, but not all of us want long term. You choose.

Let's say that your stealth advance across the room and your undeniable wit and charming approach have produced some immediate evidences of merit. Stay with it for a while, and get past the sometimes awkward stage of meeting for the first time. Relax; you have the book to get you through. Maybe he does too. In fact, that is a good opening question, "Have you read the book, The 3 C's? by that guy Pace?" Human chemistry is a feeling; you'll know it's right when it is. Molecular interactions start kicking in and we start having those giddy moments of being a child again, you know, acting stupid. If you are in a social or club setting, hopefully it's hormones not the alcohol that is taking over your brain. Feelings are from the heart. So, use your brain to make good decisions. It's what it does best when not encumbered with alcohol or emotional interferences. Lay off the alcohol, and for now, put your intellect in monitor mode by letting your feelings take the lead. As you begin talking with the person you have singled out, it will become obvious pretty quickly whether you have something in common or not. If not, go back a few paragraphs. If it's working, go with the flow. It won't need a lot of help to keep it going; it will take off on its own.

The amazing thing about this person is that he may not be the best dressed, most attractive or articulate, but he is the epitome of what you are looking for. Look at people in happy relationships. Do you wonder what they saw in each other? This is why I cautioned you not to be zeroing in on looks, money or status. If he has it, you won't even be impressed by it. If he doesn't, you won't miss it. What you now feel is beyond the superficial. It's the real stuff, so go for it.

There are discussions regarding why people in love do stupid things. It goes something like this:

The feelings we have when we fall in love are powerful and overwhelming and result in chemical changes in our brain. People don't even realize that some of the choices they are making are destructive until the consequences smack them right in the face. One example would be exorbitant trips and gifts during the dating phase. If the money is available, great; if not, you are digging a hole for which someone has to take responsibility and be accountable for. A simpler example is the couple on the phone for hours at a time and late into the night without realizing it. Job performance the next day may suffer, long distance telephone bills are excessive, etc. However, the chemistry (first "C") is on overload and sentimental comments that come out our mouths would make a baby throw up. That's one of the tests. Are you doing and saying dumb things? If so, you are chemically bonded. So far, so good. Now what? The tough stuff! If you want to stay in love with the one you are with, you have to make some hard choices, but soon you will know what the issues are. The one you may be with for the rest of your life may not be the one you are reading this book with or for.

If you graph the initial love phase of a relationship as 120%, indicating an over-the-top, no holds barred, sky-is-the-limit range of emotions, then why would you want to live the rest of your life at 50%? Fifty percent is a break-even of emotions, as many good as there are bad. I predict that you can graph the emotions of those who are followers of the 3 C's that you will live the rest of your relationship life with the person with whom you are compatible at a low of 80% yet still experience moments at that same 120% excitement. That is why it is important to follow the steps outlined in the following chapter on Compatibility. If you short cut or settle for less, you will be disappointed in yourself and the other person and have to make new decisions regarding how to undo or re-do the decision. By that time, you have joint issues to factor in, such as children, mortgages, etc. The lesson here is to be honest from the get-go, and if it works, great. If not, try again with someone else. It's not like you are fishing in a pond with just one fish.

The next chapter is where the clothes come off, and we see all the warts and scars of the other person. If you were not paying attention, he also gets to see yours. It's o.k., you are chemically attracted so you probably won't be a little bit embarrassed. A lot maybe, but not a little.

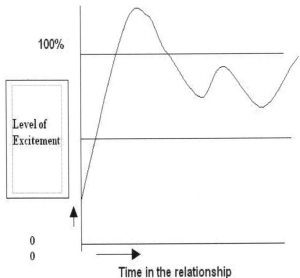

Relationship Emotions Phase Graph

100%

Level of Excitement

0
0

Time in the relationship

Time is irrelevant, days, months or years; it doesn't matter.

Notes, Questions and Conclusions
This is not a test, you cannot fail, so be honest with yourself.

_____

_____

_____

_____

_____

_____

_____

_____

_____

_____

_____

_____

_____

_____

_____

_____

_____

_____

_____

_____

_____

_____

_____

_____

_____

_____

_____

_____

_____

_____

_____

_____

_____

_____

_____

_____

_____

_____

_____

_____

_____

_____

_____

_____

_____

Chapter Five

The Second "C"

Compatibility —Not Cloning

Compatibility to many people is the same as cloning: "I have to be just like him/her; I have to like the same things." Compatibility is being able to not let the differences in each other create trigger points of dissention. The small quirk you do not like when dating may be the proverbial "straw that breaks the camel's back" years from now. Do not be afraid to be who you are as your partner will find out sooner or later. Who knows? He may like you anyway. It is an impossible burden to be someone whom we are not.

Compatibility in a relationship, as I see it, is the ability of two people with different personalities and interests to agree that they can accept those differences. They are the ones who agree to be honest on the front end of a relationship and discuss their differences. They have to be willing to lose the potential partner in the hopes of finding one that accepts them and their individual quirks, habits and nuances. One of the statements on the cover page, "Tell me what you don't like about me today because you are going to hate it in a very short time" is extremely important to keep re-asking your partner. Think about it, those of us in current or failed relationships. Wasn't it the little things that drove us crazy or to the point of chopping the person up in little meatballs, not the big things? You have to make your own list, but examples of small things that need to be discussed and agreed on as "make or break" items could be these:

For women:

- The commode lid was left up, and I fell in, again
- You did not clean your whiskers out of the sink, again
- You did not call when you were going to be late for dinner, again
- When we dated, you used to clean up on the weekends
- When we dated, you took me to plays and nice restaurants

For men:

- You never had a "headache" when we were dating.
- You were always "fixed-up" when we dated.
- You used to like my friends.
- You used to go hunting with me.

You get the idea. The list is your own, so discuss it way before, not after, the wedding. We are who we are, and we will only change if we want to and not for anyone else or as a result of any amount of threatening. Compatibility is realizing the other person's good and bothersome traits and still wanting to spend the rest of your life with him. This knowledge is crucial to know before, not after, the wedding. Once you discuss the upcoming five compatibility points, you will have a good idea, not perfect, but close enough, to say "I do", assuming you are still talking, that is.

I am sure your curiosity is overwhelming you at this point. What is he talking about? Give me something, or just shut up. Okay, you asked for it and here it is. The Five, "make or break" compatibility components are these:

1. Emotional
2. Physical
3. Intellectual
4. Spiritual
5. Sexual

Notice once again there is nothing regarding the necessity of having a great body or attractive face, high net worth, or social status to have a great relationship. It doesn't matter, and it is not necessary to possess any of those things to be happy in a relationship. It's nice if you have it, but it won't make you any happier. Your looks will surely change; you can lose your money; and social status is surely nothing on which to trust the happiness of the rest of your life, so forget about it. The 5 points above, if you are truly compatible with your partner, will be more than enough to compensate for any misguided envy you have of your neighbor's stuff. I predict that he would give it all up to be as happy as you and your partner. So him tell why you are so happy, and maybe he will let you borrow some of his stuff.

Here is the number one and only rule for taking the compatibility exam: be honest and brutal, without fudging on answers. If you are not honest, you will not be as happy as you could have been with the truly compatible person, and you will either divorce or resign yourself to the make-do life of many couples today. You see them everywhere. They don't talk, are not considerate of each other, never smile and look as though they would just as soon run their partner down using their hood ornament as a gun sight.

Know that the chemical, romantic bonding that you have enjoyed is short-lived if you are not compatible. It won't last if there is not substance to get you through the junk life throws at you—sick kids, dying parents, money issues. Now you know why you need a compatible partner. Life is tough, so get someone to stand beside you, not pushing you into the flames screaming burn, burn.

Today, after 18 years, my wife and I are frequently stopped in restaurants by wait staff and patrons and asked if we are newlyweds. We hold hands and look at each other as we talk. It is not always romantic dialogue that is ensuing, but the touch and look are the same. My wife and I are friends and respect and protect that aspect of our relationship more than most. As children, we all had our best friends and would guard that relationship with fervor. It seems as adults, we forgot that uniqueness of having someone that knows all our secrets and is trusted never to disclose to anyone those intimacies. Most of us have forgotten the penalty of "cross your heart and hope to die". Your partner needs to be your best friend and take an oath as you did when you were young. The issue of divorce and your partner's taking your secrets to the world goes away when you know that your best friend will be with you forever. It opens up a whole new set of opportunities to be open and ask for whatever comes to mind. Even if you don't get what you asked for, you at least get to ask and not worry about ridicule or judgment. Trust is what you build on in a relationship; if you don't have it, you don't have anything. The last C will make this clear to those who make it through the five compatible points and are not truthful with their partner. Don't lie. Now is the time for you to trust and be trusted. If you can't, work on your trust issues and come back, but don't go into the relationship with half-truths. If your partner judges you or is not willing to listen without criticism, you have the wrong partner. Pack up and move on. It is not yours or your partners right to do anything but listen to each other and get to know the person inside the clothes. This is fact finding at its best and worst. If you get to an impasse on one of the points, pick another, take a break or go to a movie. This is the rest of your life you are talking about. You are not in a race; make it fun; and find humor in some of your pickiness. Laugh at yourself, and if you can, laugh with your partner about himself or herself. We all want to be close, but life often beats the trust and fun out of us at an early age. Sometimes it is difficult to remember what it was like to find joy in small things. I challenge people with whom I talk to, "Remember to be childlike, not childish". Childlike is the simple enjoyment of the simple things in life; childish is stomping our feet when we don't get our way. Sometimes I have to sit back and observe a child at play and remember that I, too, used to be a child and enjoyed those same things.

For those stout in heart and willing to let it all hang out, let us go to the five compatibility points. There is no order and no weighted averages. All that matters is that you discuss each point in detail, honestly and without judging. Go back if you remember something that seems important. Remember, the third C will come back to haunt you if you don't. One other rule before you do the 5 points (okay, that's two for those of you who are counting) is that if you are having sex, you must stop. Sex clouds the truth. If you are honest, you may get tossed out anyway, so stop now and maybe it won't be so traumatic if you find out you are not the one. Better to find out now than a few years down the road when feelings of entrapment begin to really mess up the relationship. Of course there are those who won't or can't stop having sex. It's your choice, and the rest of your life with this person is dependant on the total honesty you committed to share. If you tell your sex partner his mouthwash isn't making it, and he cuts you off anyway, take your chances. I believe that time out of the bedroom is well spent in finding the right person with whom to spend the rest of your life.

Notes, Questions and Conclusions
This is not a test, you cannot fail, so be honest with yourself.

_____

_____

_____

_____

_____

_____

_____

_____

_____

_____

_____

_____

_____

_____

_____

_____

_____

_____

_____

_____

_____

Chapter Six

Emotional Compatibility

Compatibility is probably my favorite "C". As I previously mentioned, we think with our brains and feel with our hearts, so why do we let our emotions get us into so much trouble? Draw two circles side by side without them touching each other. Label one emotions; and the other, intellect (Page 56). If it were possible, we would make decisions only in this fashion. Reasoning and calculated decisions would be made without any emotions to factor in. The same is true about feelings. They could be intense without intellect telling us that we should not feel this way or that way. To really get a sense of feeling through emotions, watch a child play. They are not distracted by worry or stress; they only have the ability to enjoy what is in front of them. Another emotional area is sex. Great sex is emotional. If you are thinking about it, you are being intellectual, and that detracts from the intensity of the moment. I have read that good sex is selfish; i.e., the more you work at enjoying it for yourself, the better your partner enjoys

49

it, kind of a win-win deal. Road rage is an example of emotional behavior without intellectual boundaries. Intellectual separation prevents actions without thoughts of consequences.

I touched briefly on the emotional circle and the intellectual circle and how they should operate independently of each other. We think with our intellect and feel with our emotions. In a relationship, emotions are best when feelings of love, intimacy, and nurturing are forefront. When one is happy, that is as far as one needs to think about it. When we are unhappy, investigate as to why. Just because we are unhappy does not mean that it is someone's fault or someone's responsibility to make us happy. Investigate the source of your unhappiness; oftentimes, it is not external but internal. Second, match your feelings with the facts. Is there something that is going on with which my feelings of unhappiness match? When we laugh it is usually because something was said or a circumstance occurred that was funny; ergo, laughter. Funerals usually do not provoke a feeling of levity, so laughter is not something one hears much at funerals. This is the same thing as "owning" our own feelings. If life circumstances do not warrant your feeling of unhappiness, maybe it is chemical in nature, and an opinion of a health care provider is recommended. If circumstances or physical conditions justify the feeling of unhappiness, take a look at yourself. What are you telling yourself? If you feed yourself negative ideas about yourself or your circumstance, you will feel negative. Okay, your feelings match what you are telling yourself, but is what you are telling yourself the best thing for your well being? I am not saying these things to invalidate or minimize your feelings but to confirm that what you tell yourself is factual and necessary for your best mental state. I do not see a lot of benefit by saying "well, it could be worse," or "my friends tell me that I should not feel this way." What I am saying is, match what you tell yourself with your feelings, and confirm that the message you give yourself is factual. Is it something that I can do anything about, and where do I go from here? Depression brought on by constant dwelling in the gloom and doom of everyday life is devastating. Life is not fair. Whoever said so was telling you an untruth. What is true is that we can make the best of what we get, be grateful for the good stuff and go forward with the knowledge that one of two things will happen. It will get better, or it will get worse. Life is not static; it is always changing. What we do not know is the time between the peaks and valleys. Jumping ahead a little to Chapter 9, as a spiritual person and a Christian, I believe the tough times, which are inevitable, are easier to weather if we have something outside our conceptual understanding on which to rely. Since I have a personal frame of reference as a result of my near death experience, I choose to believe in God. It is hard not to believe in a higher power when you have had one-on-one discussions with angels, and their presence is visible. It is difficult to keep oneself on track emotionally. Throw in another human being, and the task ramps up pretty quickly. Commit to both of you not being off center at the same time, thereby giving you a human presence to confide and lean on. Don't keep score as to who gets to be dysfunctional. Just go with the one who seems to need it the most. A word of caution, don't overdo it. Keep the level of dysfunction within reasonable limits, and don't always be the one who needs the opportunity to come unwound. God is great, and he is the ultimate source of our strength. But, it is comforting at times to have a physical being you trust, someone with whom you can converse and hold. There are times when we need more than another human can provide. This is why one of the compatibility issues is spiritual. Spiritual strength is increased when shared with another believer. For the unbelievers, I do not know what you do for strength. I am not condemning or condoning, I just don't know because I do not have your beliefs. I do know that being unevenly yoked in a relationship applies both in the biblical sense and in a practical sense. You have to pull together as a couple in all relationship areas. It is difficult to impossible when that relationship is shared with a believer and a non-believer.

To effectively communicate our feelings we need to be aware of our emotional state. On page 95 of this book is a diagram of Emotional Areas Where We Live. The Venn Diagram (page 56) coupled with the Bar Diagram on page 95 provides one with a set of tools to gauge one's current emotional status. Many of us have tried to communicate our feelings only to find ourselves embroiled in conversations that took a decided turn for the worse. Instead of making things better, they became worse. Our solution oftentimes is to stop trying and keep our feelings to our self. I suggest, instead, assessing your emotional status, getting yourself in a healthy emotional place and then communicating. A third tool to use in your emotional assessment is to know where you are in the grieving process. Kubler-Ross authored the book *On Death And Dying* which identified five stages that a dying patient experiences when informed they have a terminal illness. Another resource is *Living With An Empty Chair—A Guide Through Grief* in which Kubler-Ross identifies the stages as follows:

- Denial (this is not happening to me)
- Anger (why is this happening to me)
- Bargaining or deal making (If I can live a little longer I will eat better, drink and smoke less, etc. I promise to be a better person if I can live, etc.)
- Depression (Giving up and not caring)
- Acceptance (Okay, I'm ready to accept the inevitable or whatever the grieving is about)

Dr. Roberta Temes identified three behavior types:

- Numbness (socially isolated and rote behavior)
- Disorganization (an intense and painful feeling of loss)
- Reorganization (mainstreaming back into social settings)

It has been my philosophy that in order to be able to resolve present and past losses, we must be in touch with each of the stages/types. I believe one has to acknowledge that they exist, feel whatever feelings are associated with the particular area of grieving and then move on to the next. Acceptance cannot be achieved until each stage is experienced and completed. There are situations where one must revisit a previous stage to complete the emotional recovery if he does not feel he has finished. There is no correct order, but the progression for most people is fairly consistent with those presented.

I use both authors' descriptions of the grieving process in all areas of my life in which a loss has occurred. Men are especially prone to discount a loss because it's not "manly" to admit something bothers them. Women oftentimes do not have someone with whom they can share their feelings of loss. Be conscious of all loss, whether it is your own imminent death, loss of a parent or loved one due to death or separation, your job, a divorce, or even the family pet, it is a loss. I am not suggesting you throw yourself into a pit if Fido is gone, but deal with it at the level of importance you assign to it. Only you know how important a particular loss is, so don't let someone tell you "It's not a big deal." Another overlooked facet of grieving a loss is that some losses have multiple impacts. For example, you are diagnosed with a terminal illness. Healthy people begin the grieving process and start dealing with the emotional valleys and peaks. What if your illness goes into remission? For most of us, sighs of relief and celebrations begin. What if your terminal illness comes back? One has to begin the grieving process once again and repeat the steps. The same conclusion can be reached for any loss in which multiple ends and beginnings are present within the loss.

The importance for using the three tools is to create the healthiest emotional state for oneself. If we are grieving over a loss, living in the area of anger/fear/hurt, or unable to separate our emotional/intellectual functions, we cannot effectively communicate our true feelings. Most of us remember the "Bell Curve" that indicated good, normal and unacceptable score positions. As people, we talk about being "normal." I suggest we move ourselves to the left of the Bell Curve and become healthy. Normal is where the curve is the highest and most people function. Most people are functioning dysfunctional. We learn to adapt, make the best of a situation and move on. Healthy people know who they are and their level of emotional wellness and work at keeping it. The farther we move to the right of the Bell Curve, the more dysfunctional we become. These tools are not hard to master but are important in being able to communicate your emotional status and needs to your partner.

Separation Venn Diagrams for Decision Making

Desired but not Possible

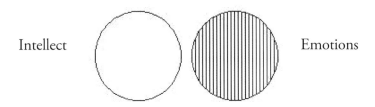

Most Effective Decision Making

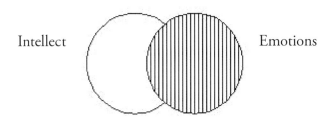

Worst Decision Making

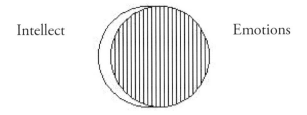

Notes, Questions and Conclusions
This is not a test, you cannot fail, so be honest with yourself.

_____

_____

_____

_____

_____

_____

_____

_____

_____

_____

_____

_____

_____

_____

_____

_____

_____

_____

_____

_____

Chapter Seven

Physical Compatibility—It's Not What You Think

We are not talking about physique, good looks, being bald or furry; physical compatibility is a function of compatible life styles. Once again, we are not talking of cloning, just awareness and acceptability. Simply stated, can you accept your partner's choices? An extreme example could be a dedicated aerobics instructor married to a couch potato. Another example could be one who watches his diet, eating a well-balanced healthy meal, coupled with one who eats anything not moving, and that, too, if it is moving slow enough. "We are what we eat" has been a catch phrase for years, and it is, to some degree, true. Heredity has some play in our ability to metabolize food allowing for a thinner body and cholesterol numbers staying in line regardless how much we ingest fat-laden foods. Overall, however, we cannot escape the fact that more calories in than out equal a rounder body shape plus greater demands on our respiratory and cardiovascular system. Exercise of any kind and duration helps to negate some of heredity's implications. I am not saying what or how much to eat or exercise, but you can figure it out by looking at the scale and the mirror (without your clothes on if you really want to know).

The problem with our personal choices of eating, drinking and exercise is that it affects everyone in your circle of influence and then radiates outward to theirs. Cancer, Alzheimer's, and other debilitating diseases do not affect just the person with the disease. An example of how one person's debilitating illness affects those around is illustrated by looking at a baby's mobile that hangs above the crib. It is impossible to touch one part of the mobile without disturbing all the others. I guess what I am saying is that we are susceptible to a lot of life-changing illnesses, some of which we can do nothing about. So, why not make intelligent life choices? In other words, if it isn't good for you, don't do it no matter how good it makes you feel for the short haul.

Anyone who is older than puberty knows of the myriad of addictive substances that are available. It should be evident that potential physical compatibility conflicts exist at many opportunities. Some studies demonstrate that certain people may be predisposed to addictive behavior. This predisposition could be physical or emotional. This chapter is not written to discuss in detail any one addictive behavior but to give you the impetus, that whether it is you or your partner, to make a conscious decision to ferret out the facts of the consequences of continuing bad life style choices. It affects you, your partner and the entire family system. Poor lifestyle choices can be compared to the baby's mobile over the crib. It is virtually impossible to move one of the pieces of the mobile without affecting the others. This is true with our good and bad life style choices; it will affect everyone, sooner or later. Find out for yourself what works for you on a physical and emotional level.

Exercise, a vital component of our physical well-being, brings with it the added benefit of something that is free, endorphins. My wife who has taught aerobics for over twenty-eight years would never speak to me if I did not extol some of the benefits of exercise; i.e., increased metabolism, increased muscle tissue toning, improved lung capacity, cardiovascular benefits, decreased junk-food cravings. These items represent a pretty good return on your time for something that you can do almost anywhere, anytime and with little or no monetary cost.

The real message I am trying to convey in this chapter can be found in the question from the first paragraph of this chapter, "Can you accept your partner's choices that impact his/her physical compatibility with yours? Statistics show that humans, as a whole, are living longer. My question is this, are we living our longer years in good health? We could be, if we do our part, and heredity does not become a factor. I personally do not want to live past any age where I am not in good health. A toast I once heard goes something like this, "May you live as long as you want, but not want as long as you live." I do not want to have to accept the inevitable consequences of someone's taking care of my needs nor me of someone else's needs if we did not exercise some prudence (surely, you think that was a mistaken pun) in our diet, exercise and addictive behavior choices. When I was young, I thought I was going to live forever; yet, I was found face down in a pond at the age of three at a family reunion, have been inside an automobile which was totaled, flew my first solo training flight during which the engine stopped running, and, of course, experienced my near death incident. I won't even mention the many other lesser invitations to "buy the farm" as western heroes used to say. As unpredictable as life is, why not up the odds by doing the things that we know will be beneficial to our health? Let's see; living longer and in good health is a great return on those odds.

Do not construe anything I have said in this chapter to mean that I *do* all the things I have written about. If I did, I would look better, feel better and live a longer, more productive life. Remember, life is about choices and subsequent consequences. I have never smoked and consume moderate amounts of alcohol, primarily wine. Remember what I said about heredity? You can't escape it. Due to a hormone deficiency and the requirement to take hormone replacement therapy, I have gained weight. Couple that with the resurgence of an old back injury that prevents me from doing my favorite exercise regimen, aerobics, I am now slightly overweight and cardiovascularly deprived. I have also contracted a chronic lung infection due in part, I believe, from a sinus infection resulting from scar tissue in my sinus cavities from the rebuilding of the right side of my facial bones. This inhibits strenuous exercise as well. My wife continues to eat well, drink in moderation and exercise daily; it is apparent to those who know her. She looks and feels great and, due to the free endorphins I mentioned earlier, has a great mental attitude.

Why am I going on about health and fitness, and what does that have to do with relationships? Nothing at all if you can accept the differences in each other's life style choices and ultimate consequences. It is your life to live as you choose, in whatever state of health or unhealth, as the case may be. What about your partner? Do you care if he exhibits careless choices? Do you want to be the one who dies prematurely (I always questioned that phrase; what is premature death because for me, any time is premature) or watch your partner struggle with the consequences of bad life style choices? We all grow older, and then we die. If you are happy with your choice of a life partner, why not make it last as long as possible to enjoy the benefits of a quality, healthy life style?

Physical compatibility also takes in the realm of non-health activities. My wife accompanied me on a fishing trip to Laguna Madre, near Corpus Christ, Texas in November the year before we married. It was cold, wet and windy. All the other wives stayed in their rooms to rise at a much later hour than 3 or 4 a.m. so they could go shopping. Judy never complained about the miserable conditions she was enduring. When we returned to the dock, I asked her, "How did you like it, and would you do it again?" After a pensive moment searching for an answer, she replied, "If you want me to, I will do it again." I then realized that here stood a person, more special than I could have imagined. The words cascaded through my frozen brain cells, and I was awed. "If I wanted her to go again, she would." Herein lies another piece of the happy lifestyle puzzle I am hoping to get you to embrace. The fact that she would go was all I really wanted to hear; no man would want to expose his partner to the rigors of the wet and cold environment unless she enjoyed the experience on its own merits. The fact that she would do it again to be with me was sufficient. I have never asked her to go again, but she would if I did and do it happily.

Men and women are hard-wired at the factory. We are different in many ways. But, we are alike in one very important way, which is the issue of trust. We may not realize on a conscious level that we have to know, no matter the outcome, what is the truth. Dating for some people is make-believe. They feel that they have to perform, look and act a certain way and then after the "I do's" can go back to who they really are. Big mistake. Know that the person to whom you are marrying may be doing the same thing to you. What a way to start out with one or both of you pretending to be someone you are not. Imagine for a moment the disappointment and feelings of betrayal that would result in the realization that some or all of the things on which you based your dating experiences are not true.

How many of us have heard our friends say, "When we were dating, he would dress up all the time and take me out." Then she finds out when confronting him that his answer is, "We were dating, I had to do those things." My wife-to-be could have said that, but she opted for a moment of polite honesty, "I would if you wanted me to." The simple act of asking and getting an honest answer avoided countless surprises and disappointments. Another story told to me concerned the girlfriend who never missed a hunting season—deer, duck, and bird. She was right in the middle of things, until, you guessed it, she married. Her answer, "I thought I had to do those things with you because we were dating." I don't get it; sooner, not later, the truth is going to come out. Most of us want to be honest, as long as it gets us what we want. What we don't want are the consequences. As much as we want to believe that we are good at lying, we are not. It eats at our core, and we drag around the horrible knowledge that the person with whom we promised to be honest is not. Stop for a moment and inventory your behavior while dating. Is it consistent with the behavior after you were married? With what half-truths did you start the relationship? Keep this inventory to yourself for the time being. If you make it to the end of the book, there will be opportunities to reclaim your role as a trustworthy person.

As you can surmise, physical compatibility is not what you thought. There is a size and shape for all of us. What I am talking about is physical compatibility and the honesty it takes to make it possible for the concept of this book to work. By now you have figured out that without honesty, nothing will last for long nor be enjoyable in the purest sense.

In an earlier chapter, I mentioned some of the "small" things that we do that irritate our partner. Remember what I said, "If it bothers you today, you are going to hate it in years to come." Ask yourself, "Am I listening to what bothers my partner?" "Is it something that I could stop doing?" "Am I doing it to annoy her?" Physical compatibility also comes in the form of knowing the nuances that bug our partner, some of which we may be aware, while others may be just our way of doing things. It is incomprehensible for me to believe that someone who truly cares for someone would deliberately antagonize his or her partner. Make your own list of what is annoying to you and maintain your position as long it takes to either understand that it is no consequence and drop it or insist that the annoyance stop. If your partner doesn't understand why it bugs you; that isn't the point. It's *your* point. Men and women have their own unique list of things they do not like. The exercise of talking about the things that bother you in a calm, mature fashion is incumbent to achieving a resolution. For women, the raised commode lid may be high on the list. For men, it may be something sexual/visual is on the list. Men are just that way, never satisfied, o.k.? This is not an attempt to be biased; it just seems that a lot of men complain about these things. I believe that if men were to follow the process of compatibility contained in this book, their complaints would disappear. For those inclined to follow the higher power route, the Bible talks of how a husband should treat his wife and how special a gift is a good wife. Husbands are to love and serve their wives unconditionally. The Bible also gives wives clear directions. Wives are to respect and follow their husbands' leadership. The biblical term, submissive, is thrown about yet misinterpreted by many. I believe that if we are with the right partner and do what we have been instructed to do, most wives would be willing to listen to our requests.

If you are compatible, the issues of the small things can be resolved. If you find out that something is important to your partner and it will not harm you or compromise your value system, just do it and quit complaining. You too have things you want. This is not compromise; this is considering the feelings of another and having the capacity and desire to do something about it. If I were a woman, I would like to have the security of sitting down in a dark bathroom and not falling into the bowl. If I were a man, a plus would be asking for a weekend of hunting without a barrage of guilt thrown at me. These are just examples; do your own list, and talk it over. If you take care of the small things, there will not be any big things to deal with.

Notes, Questions and Conclusions
This is not a test, you cannot fail, so be honest with yourself.

_____

_____

_____

_____

_____

_____

_____

_____

_____

_____

_____

_____

_____

_____

_____

_____

_____

_____

_____

_____

_____

Chapter Eight

Intellectual Compatibility— Book vs. Street Smarts

H ow long does it take you to run out of things to talk about with your partner? If you are already out, read on; if you are not out, read on anyway.

The ability to communicate is not just a function of intelligence but also a function of compatibility and sincerity. The longevity question asked in the first paragraph is also a function of compatibility. To be able to talk to someone for years and years of married life and still look forward to more opportunities to share information, anecdotes and stories is extremely important. At your next opportunity, look around at the people sitting at the tables in a restaurant. Is anyone talking? Is anyone *really* listening? A conversation takes *two* people, as well as the exchange of information. So what I am saying to do is to ask yourself "What am I hearing?" and "Does my listener's response confirm for me that what he heard is what I said?"

Intellectual compatibility is not defined by communications skills but through a series of interpersonal devices unable to be quantified. Touch, feel, smell, visual and aural cues are forms of intellectual compatibility. IQ in itself is a quantifiable number predicated on tests and responses. Communication skills and compatibility require IQ, not as the sole indicator, but as a compatibility indicator. How many of us have finished our partner's sentence or made the same comment at the same time? Intellectual compatibility, when successful, is a great thing as are the other four compatibility issues. Intellectual compatibility gives a couple the benefit of being able to talk or discuss a myriad of topics over a long period of time without being bored or irritated. In fact, we are stimulated by the opportunity to discuss open and sometimes opposing concepts with our partner. Someone with the IQ of a Mensa member trying to discuss abstract concepts with a below functioning IQ could perhaps define the worst case of intellectual compatibility. The high IQ individual would become frustrated with the other person's lack of ability to understand the seemingly simple concepts of relativity while the other person would just as easily tire of being bombarded with words and phrases that do not have any semblance of real words. Herein lies the conflict: "Why aren't you listening to me?" or "Why don't you understand what I am saying?" asks the self-appointed master of the conversation while the recipient of the lecture is fending for his life. The recipient may respond with "Why don't you speak with words I understand?" or "Why are you talking down to me?" Something has got to give in this situation; both parties are unhappy with the inability to communicate, and both feel denied the opportunity to have a meaningful conversation. If they stay together, the conversations will diminish in quality and quantity. In addition, resentments on both sides will grow and further diminish the desire to share any intellectual property each may have to share. Low IQ does not equate to dull or without merit. The continued emphasis of this book is to stress the importance of compatibility. My wife was college valedictorian and achieved all A's (except for one B in freshman orientation) pursuing a degree in math. I, on the other hand, struggled for A's from the beginning in my quest for a degree in engineering. I, of course, attribute that to my working full time and trying to go to school full time, not a lack of brainpower. The point is that we were both smart enough to graduate from college. I believe that she is probably smarter than me if we went toe-to-toe on IQ tests. That is not important. What is important is that we are intellectually compatible. We talked for hours when we started dating and still do some twenty-four years later. Our conversations range from her latest exercise class routine to current events. We never tire of each other's conversation. Perhaps the decision not to engage in gossip or dwelling on the misfortunes of others or our own has contributed to our continued desire and ability to be intellectually communicative.

Intellectual compatibility comes into focus when one knows when to shut up and listen. No one keeps score on who is right or talks the most. Our conversations are simply that, an exchange of information with personal filtering kept to a minimum. I don't like nor do I try to have information filtered. Tell me just like you read or heard it; I can take it from there. There are times when no one has to talk; sometimes talking gets in the way of communicating through touching or looking.

Intellectual compatibility requires the ability to recognize the differences in each other. The ability to gauge emotional coping skills, communication skills, one's desire to feel safe, etc., is part of intellectual compatibility. Intellectual compatibility goes beyond the IQ number; it is also the ability to know what to do, how to do it and when to do it. Sometimes it is important to listen for what is not being said; inquire, but don't intrude. I obviously like to talk, and that is why you are reading this book; my hope is that it will be of benefit to someone, to save a relationship or help in finding one that fulfills both parties' needs and wants. Judy was not a talker, and it was difficult for us to communicate during conflict. She has overcome that issue and now can hold her own when conflict arises.

There are two kinds of "smarts" in my concept of intellectual compatibility. One is the IQ smart; the other is street smart. We have all met extremely intelligent people only to leave the conversation hoping they have the ability to find their way out of the building. Others stumble over words and concepts but have been educated in the so-called "hard knocks of life." We need both, and, hopefully, what we lack in one our partner will fill in the gaps for the other. We all can't be rocket scientists, so one must have a little compassion for those less intellectually endowed; after all, someone has to build the rocket.

Notes, Questions and Conclusions

This is not a test, you cannot fail, so be honest with yourself.

_____

_____

_____

_____

_____

_____

_____

_____

_____

_____

_____

_____

_____

_____

_____

_____

_____

_____

_____

_____

_____

Chapter Nine

Spiritual Compatibility— Believers and Non-believers

Let me begin by saying that I do not want to offend anyone regarding his or her spiritual bias. I want to remind you that this book is about compatibility, not religious preferences.

My concept of God is admittedly skewed; having had a near-death experience, I am convinced that angels and God exist. I am equally convinced that the counterparts, forces of evil, also exist. I was given a second chance for reasons I do not know but hope to discover on my second trip to eternity. For me, I always felt comfortable with the concept of religious beliefs. I do not have any prejudice against any other form of religion or a person's decision to go it alone. This is my belief, and I have asked for guidance from God in writing this book. This is who I am. Don't beat me up; I won't you, either.

Spiritual compatibility is similar in concept to that of intellectual compatibility. You have to have a frame of reference to share the experience. A relationship between a hardcore Bible-thumping Christian and a hardcore atheist will be, in my opinion, tumultuous and contentious. How is this going to be a compatible issue in any shape or form? One party is going to be sniping at the other to come over to his side. Throw children into the mix, and then the party really gets wild.

As I said earlier, I am not going to quote Bible verses or engage any other form of religious interrogatories or edicts. Consider what you will, and be open-minded. The issue at hand is not about conversion but about being compatible with your partner, and to some extent, your fellowship with the rest of the population. Morality, the concept of right and wrong, for some is founded in spiritual beliefs. It is my understanding that individuals who are discovered in remote locations have a sense of right and wrong. So what's up? Where do they get this sense of it's wrong to kill except in self-defense or steal from someone? I have my ideas; go out and develop your own.

My father was not a practicing believer until a few days before his death. At that time he chose to be "born again" as the concept is worded today. The phrase "There are no atheists in fox holes" probably came about from a soldier who decided to hedge his bet that, "If I die, I'm not taking any chances. What have I got to lose?"

When I use the word, the Bible, it is not intended to disallow other books of religious beliefs, the Koran, the Book of Mormon, etc. Whatever your discipline is, ask the guy in charge to give you not just the wisdom but also the discernment to know what is morally right. Wisdom without discernment is about being half-right.

My reference is the Bible; I am sure your spiritual guidebook or leader has words of wisdom that you follow. Having said that, the Bible talks of being "unevenly yoked." In the practical sense, oxen were used to pull wagons and in other forms of labor; therefore, it was important for two or more animals to be equal in strength, attitude and, to some extent, innate intelligence. If the animals were not evenly yoked, the wagon, plow or whatever was hooked to them had a tendency to get crooked or stall, causing delays, and accidents or, in another words, they just made a big mess of things. Ergo, we human beings come under the same criteria; i.e., if we are not equal, "evenly yoked," in the proper amount and in similar things, our lives become a hodge-podge of conflict, discord and general unhappiness.

I grew up with the belief that man will let you down, but God (your higher power) will not. The problem with that concept is that it requires faith. Most of us like to be able to wrap our hands around a problem to get a sense of the magnitude and significance of its presence. There is no such luck with faith-based prayer. You just have to give it up and know that the best for you will be in the works. The problem is that we want answers now. We oftentimes do get a fairly quick answer; it is one of three, yes (my favorite), no (my least favorite), and not now (my most misunderstood). With spiritual compatibility, the wait time for not now and the time making new plans when we surmise that the answer is the dreaded no, feels shorter and is much more bearable.

Once again, the task set out in this book is to answer the question of compatibility. Are you able to communicate your religious preferences in an honest manner so that at some future point in the relationship your partner cannot say, "You didn't tell me that!" The reason for total honesty in religious compatibility, like the other four, is to establish trust with one another. If you hold back, or do not discuss with full disclosure your honest feelings, it is only a matter of time before the relationship will begin to suffer. It does not make any difference what compatibility issue causes the relationship to fail. I have said earlier and will say it again, each person has to be willing to face the termination of the relationship upon determination that the information received is not acceptable to his or her individual goals for the relationship. As painful as it sounds, it is better to stop now than continue viewing him as a potential life partner. You can always just be friends.

Spiritual compatibility includes such practicalities as "Where do you want to go to church?" or "Do we pray together?" or "I do not have any beliefs, and I do not want to be with someone who does." Take a deep breath and be prepared; remember, there is someone out there who is looking for you, so don't sell your spiritual values short.

Notes, Questions and Conclusions

This is not a test, you cannot fail, so be honest with yourself.

_____

_____

_____

_____

_____

_____

_____

_____

_____

_____

_____

_____

_____

_____

_____

_____

_____

_____

_____

Chapter Ten

Sexual Compatibility

The Easy One

I say "easy" because if you have established a truly compatible relationship with your partner based on the preceding four compatibility topics and have been honest with your self and your partner, you are going to love this part. If you have not been honest with either yourself or your partner, the next "C" will offer you an opportunity to do so.

There have been a lot of books written on the subject of sex, from both a man's perspective and a woman's, and none address the issue of compatibility that I am aware of. Far from a sex expert, I have been in enough experiences and listened to a plethora of complaints regarding sex from both men and women to know that there is way too much grief surrounding sex. Sex, in my opinion, has been commercialized and shoved in our faces by special agenda groups for years. Granted, for years it was relinquished to simply an act of procreation for some, and for some, still is. But in reality, it should be spontaneous, fun and enjoyable, regardless of how old you think you are.

Really great sex comes from total abandonment of intellectual thoughts. Earlier in the book I gave the example of drawing two circles, one for intellectual and one for emotional. Sex is that area where you can abandon intellectual thought processes and revel in the emotions of the moment. For me, sex consists of three phases, anticipation, execution, and recovery. One of my acquaintances told me one time that he was fed up with all the work that went in to something that lasted five minutes. He was not taking into account the opportunities for anticipation and subsequent benefits for his partner and himself. Execution is what you make of it. If you feel you need some tips, get a book on sex to help you figure it out. I suggest you go with the moment and be spontaneous. Recovery is the euphoria of the preceding moments continuing to distract you from the real world. Once again, don't skip any one of the three, they are all important.

Good sex cannot save a bad marriage, but bad sex can ruin a good marriage. I say that with the caveat that asks the question: "What is bad sex?" What I propose is that sex between incompatible people will come across as bad. It is not the sex as much as it is the other four compatibility issues, emotional, intellectual, physical and spiritual. Take sex out of the equation, and put yourself in a situation with business or social friends that you do not know very well or do not trust. You do not feel at ease in their presence, don't know what to say and look for ways to distance yourself from them. Fast forward to your partner. Do you trust him/her? Are there unresolved emotional issues? Is the issue of spirituality with that person where it needs to be for you? Is he abusing his body with drugs, etc? How are you supposed to let yourself go into the emotional area of your consciousness with all that stuff buzzing around?

Now is the time to be specific as you have been in the previous four components. Earlier in the book you were asked to do this in order to be more conscious of your real feelings. If you were having sex, you have mutually agreed to stop. Most of us, after attaining a few years of sexual maturity, think we know what sex is about anyway. Another agreement you and your partner need to reach is that neither of you have ever had sex before, with anyone. It may seem strange to admit that fact with several failed marriages and a bookshelf of children's photographs in plain view, but think about it. Do you really want to know anything about your future partner's past sexual experiences? No way. It is time to have some form of sexual lobotomy and go forward on the basis that you can figure out your sexual compatibility together.

Hopefully by now, you and your prospective partner are feeling pretty compatible. The first four hurdles have been accomplished, and now the finish line is staring you in the face. Yet so many of us are afraid to talk about sex to our partner; some will give intimate details to friends trying to get validation or confirmation of his/her sexual thoughts for what should be the most intimate part of a couple's relationship. What makes you think they have it figured out? You might as well read directions off the bathroom stall walls if you want advice. Remember, we are all different, including our sexuality. What you want is the person whose sexuality is compatible with yours.

Someone has to go first so it might as well be you. You have already agreed not to be judgmental, snicker or make faces, and you sure aren't going to discuss this with your friends, so what have you got to lose? Now is the time to speak up and not worry about being weird or strange. If you want chocolate syrup poured over you then rolled in Cheerios, that's who you are. Speak up. Who knows? Maybe he will bring whipped cream. As always, good sense should prevail, so keep your fun to yourself. The neighbors can make do without watching you through the open windows; keep the fun to yourselves.

Remember the childlike vs. childish behavior patterns. Sex is an opportunity to be a little childish. When trust is in place and the other four components of compatibility are a fixture in your relationship, it is time to enjoy yourself with the abandonment of a little child at play.

Still don't get it? O.K., here are a few pointers to get you started. You have to come up with the rest. You can do it; make it a fun experience. This is not the end, only the beginning of getting to know each other in the arena of intimacy. The conversation could begin with: "How do you feel about leaving the lights on/off?" "How about clothes on/clothes off?" or for the self-assured, "I always wanted to ____." The partner who is listening responds with non-judgmental answers or suggestions of his own. The conversation soon takes on a life of its own. Let it go where it wants to. Be reminded, neither of you have ever had sex, so you have to speak in terms of the unknown. Now is the time to forget any past bad experiences and try a more uninhibited approach. If you are not sure, say so. "No" is pretty final. So perhaps a "maybe" will keep the dialogue going. When my wife asked me, I came up with what I thought was the grand daddy of all answers, "I will be open to anything but three things." "No groups, drugs or animals." Needless to say, she was caught off guard, and the tension of the subject was definitely broken.

Notes, Questions and Conclusions

This is not a test, you cannot fail, so be honest with yourself.

Chapter Eleven

Consistency—The Final "C"

Consistency represents a trait often desired but seldom achieved. For example, good golfers have a consistent swing, renowned chefs consistently duplicate award winning recipes, parental training stresses consistent parental behavior and so on. In the context of this book, consistency in one's behavior results in limiting the confusion found in relationships where consistency is not practiced. The importance of honesty in discussing the five compatibility elements is one of the keys to consistent behavior. In an earlier chapter, you were given an opportunity to revise or add any truisms you shared with your partner. Now is that time for both of you to be as honest as you can, for after this opportunity passes, there will be consequences for less than full disclosure. The person with whom you are performing this exercise is depending upon you to be the person you say you are, and you upon him. Concern yourself only with your clarifications, not that of your partner. It is not surprising that either or both of you need to do some recanting. How often do we get a chance to speak of our wants, desires and feelings without the fear of judgmental or persecution backlash?

Truthfulness is the foundation of trust. It follows then that consistency is the foundation upon which we base our trust in our partner. Trust gives each partner the benefit of realistic expectations. Reasonable expectations allow clichés such as "both pulling on the same end of the rope" and "everyone rowing the same direction" to be acted out and give both parties the opportunity to achieve the same goal. Reasonable is a subjective word, and I try to avoid subjective wording. Why limit your goals or expectations? With truthfulness and trust, subjective language becomes meaningless.

I know people who are very consistent and are quick to point out those consistencies. One is my wife. She is not a morning person, never has been and probably never will be. This was one of her soul-bearing confessions during the discussion phase of the compatibility elements. I, on the other hand and unfortunately for my wife, am a morning person. Remember what was said earlier? We want to be compatible, not cloned. I have absolutely no excuse to be upset when I wake up and try to establish early morning chitchat with my wife. Of course, early morning is subjective and is up to the person being nudged into consciousness to determine the definition of "early morning." It might be of interest to note that definitions seem to change at the convenience of the definition producer. In this case, the producer does not observe consistency. It is a type of self-imposed and unwarranted free throw.

Oftentimes, a smart person can be described in the statement of a great actor, "A man has to know his limitations." Before I am criticized as an un-thoughtful husband, I will go on the record as saying that I can tell when she is truly in need of an extra two or three, or four or five whacks at the snooze button and when she is enjoying the playfulness of someone who cares about her. I do not always, but do attempt to make an earnest attempt to be thoughtful and considerate. In her way she is consistent, and I am in mine. Anything can be playful if you both try.

Two important areas of consistency for me are to never go to bed angry and to finish the issue forever (remember, when it's over, it's over). When the dust settles and the bandages are on, the truce is in place (there is no winner if you have ever noticed, only losers). It is time to get back to the area of your relationship where you both feel loved, secure, and protected. I will talk more of this later in this chapter. Do not go to sleep harboring any resentment or anger. If you go to bed as Ms. Bo Peep or Mr. Suave, don't wake up as Attila the Hun. It is not fair to your partner. Trust is lost, and emotional scars take their place. Enough scarring can prevent any hope of maintaining or, for that matter, recovering the uniqueness of the relationship you shared.

Let's talk for a minute about the areas in which we want to live a consistent life with our partner. If you draw a line from left to right on a piece of paper and then another line approximately two inches parallel to the first followed by a third parallel line about one-half inch from the second line you will have your life graph (Page 95). Label the area between the first and second parallel lines as Love. The small space between the second and third parallel lines is labeled Threat to You or

Someone You Care About; the space above the second parallel line is labeled Anger/Fight or Flight. Most of us are happy in the area labeled Love/Intimacy. The human mind cannot tolerate spending much time in the space labeled Threat. The large space above Threat, labeled Anger/Fear/Hurt, should be pretty recognizable to most of us because we spend far too much time in it. It is impossible to rectify or establish a resolution to a conflict from any place on the graph except in the area labeled Love/Intimacy.

Think about it. If you walk into your yard and a tiger is standing there looking at you and licking its chops, you are going to move directly into the small area of the graph labeled Threat. You will quickly then decide if you are going to fight or flee, and no one is going to be able to have a discussion with you about anything until you feel safe once again. Relationships are the same way. Until the party who feels threatened feels safe, he is not going to respond to anything you have to offer unless you remove the feeling of his being threatened. Most of us forget that we have a choice of whether to fight or return to love. Love, in this context, is not the physical arena but rather the emotional position that allows one to communicate with another to resolve the conflict at hand. Part of conflict resolution is the ability to recognize why the person is feeling threatened and to get him to move from the feeling of being threatened and mentally move to the area of Love, not Anger.

One cannot communicate (receive or give information) in any area but Love/Intimacy. If there are unsolved areas in our past, there will be overwhelming, possibly overpowering or even out of control, feelings associated with the current feeling. In order to live in only present day feelings, we need to go back to the memory of that earliest overpowering feeling from the past to establish the beginning. All feelings after the

Emotional Areas Where We Live
Anger—We attack the other person Fear—Afraid of being attacked Hurt—Our spirit is wounded
Threat to you or someone you care about
Love/Intimacy(Peaceful feelings)

beginning are simply repeats. In other words, there are not thousands of those overpowering feelings, only a few. But due to the repetitive nature, it seems like so many.

There are many reasons why conflicts are not resolved. One is the notion that one party has to win. I suggest that whether it be with your partner, family members, friends or work associates, establish the mind set that it is not about winning but about resolution. This is one of the reasons why it is important that we fight fair in order to minimize the scarring and bruising of our opponent. The truth is not always pleasant to hear. Remember from Chapter One, the truth is the one thing that will resolve any conflict. No one wins an argument about opinions—opinions are like noses; everyone has one, and they are all different. The next chapter will hopefully help you see why some of us never get back to being as happy, close or intimate as we once were. Those opportunities come about through working on symptom vs. problem recognition, and then resolution occurs using the tools we discussed earlier in this book and those from other resources that work for you.

Notes, Questions and Conclusions

This is not a test, you cannot fail, so be honest with yourself.

_____

_____

_____

_____

_____

_____

_____

_____

_____

_____

_____

_____

_____

_____

_____

_____

_____

_____

_____

_____

_____

_____

Chapter Twelve

Symptoms or Problems?

When we have a headache, we sometimes take an aspirin. If it goes away, that's the end of it. What if it doesn't? We can take stronger aspirin, pain reliever derivatives, or maybe ignore it hoping it will go away. A pain signals us that something is wrong. If the pain persists, it usually means that it is associated with a more complex and possibly serious problem. The example I used is a headache. If time and/or over-the-counter medications do not resolve the pain, there may be something more serious causing the chronic headache. A visit to your health care provider will usually determine the cause of the pain (symptom). Once the root cause of the pain is identified, corrective measures can be taken to eliminate the cause of the pain, the problem. Why is your relationship any different? It is now time to have relationship symptoms vs. relationship problems come to the front of the class. We struggle for years in a relationship not realizing that we are dealing with symptoms when we actually need to be dealing with the problem. Returning to the example of the headache, we know that aspirin will not stop a headache caused by any number of underlying conditions, tumors, vascular, stress, chemical abuse/imbalance, etc. It should be now evident that if you are in interpersonal conflict, dealing with the relationship symptoms will not cure the root cause of the relationship problem(s).

Dealing with the root cause of the conflict (the problem) eliminates the symptomatic issues as removing a brain tumor will hopefully eliminate the cause for your headache. Since we often get focused on symptoms, step back and ask yourself, "What is really going on here? We have talked about this many times and thought it was solved, but the issue keeps coming back." Life conflicts are like snapshots in time. If we look at the conflict snapshots, they will be the same picture; we just have on different clothes and look a little older.

Emotional pain like physical pain does not go away unless we do something about the problem. Just like physical symptoms that remain untreated, relationship symptoms only migrate into bigger problems and ultimately, as in our physical sense, the relationship dies, becomes impaired or exists in a catatonic state.

In my discussions with people while gathering information with which to write this book, I have been asked why I do not list money as one of the compatibility issues. It is my position that if you are emotionally, intellectually and spiritually compatible, money or the absence thereof will not be a source of conflict. Money issues are the symptom, not the problem. We all know people that are happy with or without money, as well as those who are unhappy with or without money. The difference is compatibility, not money. There is obviously an unresolved root problem causing the discord in the relationship. This unresolved problem manifests itself through symptoms of discord; trust me, it's not the money. Money for some people is how they keep score; for others, an opportunity to do good for others. Having money or not is not the reason to be happy or sad.

Earlier in the book I stated that small things should not evolve into big things. This can be paraphrased by saying symptoms do not grow into problems, but problems do create symptoms. I talked earlier of cleaning the emotional blackboard daily of irritations and of leaving no item unresolved, even if the resolution takes you into the early morning hours. This will only work if you are talking about the problems. Conflict resolution is about problem resolution, not symptom resolution. Nothing is gained haranguing each other about symptoms.

Take an inventory about which you and your partner, sibling or associates are in conflict. Chances are it is symptomatic of something that may or not be related to the discussion. If it is, you probably have a better chance of determining the problem. Often times, it is not related, and the task becomes much harder. Always go back to the first snapshot of the train wreck, see why it left the track; that's when the symptoms started and will continue until you resolve the problem.

If both parties dealing with a conflict are willing to remain unemotional and discuss the truth regarding the dispute, the task of problem detection is much more simplified. To be effective, one party must be willing to remain calm and focused while the other person is perhaps bouncing off the walls. Someone needs to be able to keep the facts straight and focus on the truth. As a reminder, there is only one truth but many opinions. Simply stated, don't both of you be mad at the same time. Although not easy to do, it can be done and usually with a successful resolution. Detaching yourself from the fray is a useful tool. The word is detached, not disinterested. Your partner can tell the difference.

A relationship that has endured years of arguing, isolationism and indifference requires much work. Go back to the beginning when you met; afterwards, something went off the track. Go back to your earliest recollection of your first conflict, and pull the pieces back together. When you say to yourself, "I can't believe I am in a relationship with this person," believe it, you are. Find out why you both got together and what went wrong along the way. It will be difficult at first but worth it if there is anything left to salvage. There are many books on this subject, so read what has worked for other couples and give it a try. Do not expect the other person to surrender; work on your contribution to the mess, and ask your partner to do the same. Stay away from blame, as well as accepting all the responsibility. Be willing to listen to the other person even if he is wrong about some of the facts. It is his reality, so be polite. A person's concept of reality is changed only through the presentation of the truth supported by facts. There is a lot of psycho-talk today about responsibility and accountability. Why not take that advice and each of you be responsible for your actions and accountable for the consequences? Radical idea.

This book is full of tips and advice all from people who didn't know I was more than just a little interested. One pearl of wisdom was the advice to enjoy being happy and only work on the things that make you unhappy. Many of us feel guilty when we are happy. We think we don't have the right to be happy when we think of the homeless, toxic waste, crime and the ever present, naval lint. There is a time for that, but your task is to keep gloom and doom thoughts within bounds. There is nothing wrong with happy—enjoy it, savor it and protect it. Something will surely come along that warrants your attention, and your focus on the positive will be taken away. In other words, don't go looking for reasons to be unhappy. There are plenty, and they will find you soon enough. The good news is that the relationship with the right partner is rewarding, even during the worst of outside influences.

Notes, Questions and Conclusions

This is not a test, you cannot fail, so be honest with yourself.

_____

_____

_____

_____

_____

_____

_____

_____

_____

_____

_____

_____

_____

_____

_____

_____

_____

_____

_____

_____

Chapter 13

The Beach is Always Sandy— Deal With It

We talk about the behavior we don't like in regard to the people in our lives. We listen to others talk about behavior they don't like about people in their life. Why do we do this? Do we really think they are going to change as a result of our commentaries? Are we so omnipotent that we know what is best? The answer to these questions and similar other questions is no. All we do is take on the reputation of being a nag and a complainer. This is the important reason for knowing early on that we can or cannot deal with the particular nuances of the person with whom we have chosen to spend what is, hopefully, the rest of our life. Early in this book we talked about change. You can only change yourself. It is pretty egotistical to think you have the power to change someone else. One will only change if he wants to and only then if he sees a reason to change. You may be thinking, "No, I know I have changed my partner." You are deluding yourself. If he changed, it was because he wanted to. If he changed for any other reason, be prepared for dynamics of resentment and regression to creep into the relationship.

Yes, "The beach is always sandy." What does all this rhetoric have to do with a sandy beach? Everything. When you plan a trip to the beach there is little concern regarding the environmental impact to yourself regarding where you are going. Have you ever arrived at the beach to immediately start complaining, "It's hot, it's sandy, and the water is salty"? I would have to believe with almost absolute certainty that it is usually hot at the beach, the beach has always been sandy, and salt water is always salty. So why do we complain? Nothing is going to change. Nothing you say will alter the heat index, the irritations of the sand or the salt content of the water. You know all these things before you left the house. Yet, here you are, fussing about something you already knew. It has to make you wonder if we were dropped on our heads as babies.

Are you starting to get it? The person about whom you have been fussing is no different than the beach. You had to have been asleep to not know the individual you are with is hot, sandy and salty after the initial hand holding period. So now you're at the beach and complaining. Good luck.

What should you do? First, stop complaining; you are only making it worse. Second, is it possible to enjoy the beach with the heat, sand and salt water? Sure it is, millions of people do it every year. The difference is your attitude. Before you jump up and down and tell yourself how tolerant and understanding you are, and it's all the other person's fault, think about the absurdity of that concept. Earlier in the book I talked about symptoms creating problems. Is this the case? Are you focusing on this person's behavior as a result of something hurtful he might have said or done that has gone unreconciled? If so, he can never do anything right in your eyes. The importance of erasing the board of one's transgressions periodically cannot be overstated. I ask my wife periodically, "What have I done that I have not taken care of?" Hopefully, she knows that whatever I did was done accidentally and without malice. It was simply a mistake, an oversight; you know, my being stupid. Doing this periodically eliminates the latent resentment that builds up when mistakes are made and not rectified.

Now, let's go back to the beach. It is my belief that if you clean your personal board of resentments and pent-up hostilities, the beach will not be as sandy; it may be acceptable and thus allow enjoyment to be possible. There is always the possibility that the person who is the object of your interest is a veritable sand dune, and no matter how hard you try you just cannot enjoy the beach anymore. Now what? I suggest that you set time aside and try starting over. Go back to the time you met. After all, he was desirable at some time, so try a do over. You probably did not have the benefit of the steps in this book to help you, so use the tools and techniques contained in the chapters to get it right this time. As life has already taught you, there are no guarantees, but what have you got to lose? You are already vested in the relationship, so maybe with a little tweaking and possible commitment to changing certain behaviors you would not have to start over. I am sure you remember how much fun kissing all those frogs and frogettes was.

In closing, most of the things that irritate us come from something we are unhappy about in our own lives. We like to think we are in control, but in reality, we have very little control over anything but ourselves. So, look to yourself first, then to external irritants.

Notes, Questions and Conclusions

This is not a test, you cannot fail, so be honest with yourself.

_____

_____

_____

_____

_____

_____

_____

_____

_____

_____

_____

_____

_____

_____

_____

_____

_____

_____

_____

_____

_____

_____

_____

Chapter 14

Gender Role Models

The only reason this chapter is in this book is to increase your awareness that your parents had a significant role in establishing who you are and the choices you make. The following are a few sample sets:

1. Traditional family unit with Father and Mother;
2. Parent divorced or deceased, child living with Mom/Dad as single parent;
3. Parent who has re-married, child living between two residences;
4. Parents who are same-sex and adopt or bring same-sex life-partner into existing single person family unit setting.

I do not possess the skills to address any of these or other subsets in detail and will only discuss them briefly to allow you the opportunity to explore your childhood memories and possibly be aware of how your behavior may be influenced. We all have a past, how you use it is up to you.

I see myself jumping into the fire, but I believe that the male/ husband should be the head-of-the-family. Before you begin sticking pins in dolls patterned after my likeness, allow me to explain. Those who subscribe to biblical/spiritual teachings have been taught that the man is the head of the household. It does not say that he is King, Ruler, Dictator or The Omnipotent One. He just has the responsibility to take the hits if something goes wrong in spite of his best intentions. The wife is also given spiritual talents, those that men do not possess. One is the gift of intuition. My wife has felt a presence of bad feelings on business deals that I have been in, and had I known (she did not tell me until after the fact) I, we, would have been much better off. I encourage her to tell me when those feelings occur. At least, if I still jump off the bridge, she can say, "I told you so." Men have too long not listened to the advice of their wives. Neanderthal, macho or lone wolf attitudes are not appreciated in a partnership. Now before the men start looking for a rope to hang the doll that looks like me, listen up. We are not given some special talent to be right. It is our responsibility to do the best we can, get a few kudos when we are right and a few aw shucks when we are wrong from our partner. The problem is that someone has to make the final decision. That is where the standing tall part comes in. If you make the call and wipe out the family fortune, it helps if you have the support of your partner in the initial decision. This is not blame, but sharing the moment of decision and using the best of you skill set to go forward.

What am I saying, and where are we going? Gender role models. We are the product of heredity and environment as I wrote earlier. Observations over the years have enabled me to write this book and also have led me to another observation. "You either marry someone just like your parent or someone totally opposite". Girls marry men that mirror their father or someone totally opposite. Men gravitate to women in the same fashion. So, what's the big deal? Let me share a few scenarios with you.

Passive father— Strong-willed mother or mirror opposite:

Men who grew up in this environment and marry passive women may have a tendency to be over-bearing husbands. They are, in some unconscious way, getting back at their mother and, perhaps, evening the score for their dad.

Strong-willed women who grew up in this environment and marry a passive male may continue the pattern set by their mothers, domineering and assuming the alpha role. The passive male wants to keep peace and declines to engage in any activity that can result in discord and be construed to be argumentative.

Strong-willed men often get carried away with the "Me-Tarzan, You-Jane" role. Relationships are not about exerting your will and dominion over another. Be a provider and protector, not a bully. Obtain respect the old-fashioned way, by earning it.

Passive women who marry strong willed men eventually lose who they were. They have no opportunity to express themselves and through atrophy, morph into someone they think they need to be to keep peace in the family. Problem is, it does not work for a variety of reasons. We are who we are, and our subconscious will be screaming to be let out. Without purpose, life is not much fun.

Both are bad plans. No one likes to be one-down or on the defense constantly. We've seen relationships where all four of these scenarios have been apparent, so shape up and save your relationship.

Passive father—Passive mother:

Men or women who grow up in this environment and marry passive partners may find themselves in a very civilized relationship, possibly boring, but civilized. I am not advocating someone has to run around beating his or her chest, but let's have a little difference of opinion once in a while. The problem is that no one is willing to speak up for fear of creating a conflict. Just because you speak up, it does not mean breaking out the gloves and going to the mat. If you are in this type of relationship, venture outside your comfort zone a little at a time. Once you have decided to discuss issues you have been thinking about, you may want to forewarn your partner about what you are going to do; no one likes this type of surprise. Repressed feelings can sometimes flow outward with the velocity of a bursting dam. Hopefully, with a little practice, discussions of opposite viewpoints can be held, and soon you're having guacamole instead of tapioca.

Strong-willed father— Strong-willed mother, or mirror opposite:

Men or women who choose to marry another strong willed individual may have a fight-to-the-death scenario because no one wants to back off. Relationships are not about winning; they're about picking the best course of action that provides the desired results. We should not be keeping score anyway. What do you win? So what if you get your way every time, big deal. Common sense should tell you that no one is always right. The important thing is working together to resolve issues, not keeping score.

This is a very simplistic view about a very complex array of dynamics; it is offered to provide you the impetus to find out more about your development during your formative years. I personally believe we should never stop learning, and we should never leave our formative years; but that's me. A day without learning something is a day wasted. That day could have given me the opportunity to learn to be a better husband to my wife, a partner in business, a parent and spiritual witness.

Notes, Questions and Conclusions

This is not a test, you cannot fail, so be honest with yourself.

_____

_____

_____

_____

_____

_____

_____

_____

_____

_____

_____

_____

_____

_____

_____

_____

_____

_____

_____

_____

Chapter 15

Cut Your Partner a Little Slack

In the course of human events, nothing seems to compare to the joys and frustrations of interpersonal relationships. We have discussed the fact that some people do not feel the need for a life partner, and that's a personal choice that one makes based on values that work for them. The rest of us, however, seem to feel more complete with a life partner. The Bible addresses this fact when Paul discusses this issue saying that for some it's okay, but for others, if you are not content, seek out a life partner.

For those who are unhappy in their relationship: Why can't we remember how happy we were in the beginning of the relationship? What happened? Why are we so unhappy?

I submit to you that if one or more of the five compatibility items is awry, the relationship is possibly terminal, but maybe not. So get out your compatibility list and check it out. Once you are at least civil to each other again, work on finding out why the relationship suffered for the length it did before you took remedial steps to fix it.

It sounds like a cliché, but life is too short to be unhappy, especially when you are in the honeymoon portion of the relationship. This is the phase when nothing should be problematic. As unpopular as it may sound, if you are early in the dating relationship and in constant discord, quit the relationship and move on. Remember, if you don't like the person or some of his behaviors now, you are really going to hate him, it or both later. Why wait? The last time I checked, you weren't getting any younger. If you are married, step back and use the tools provided in this book to see what element (s) of the relationship is out of whack. Remember, it may be you, so don't start looking at your partner like he is the problem. I would guess that in many instances, it is you or some facet of your behavior that is driving your partner nuts. If that is the fact, then the obvious issue in my mind would be to question his sanity as to why he sticks around.

Tolerance, not compromise, is a way to put you in the other person's shoes. Sometimes we all need a little slack; just don't overdo it. Nobody likes to be the one who has to always understand that his partner had a bad hair day, PMS, unrealistic co-workers or demanding supervisors. To keep it fair for the ladies, a Neanderthal for a husband, whining about not going out with the boys, etc. It works both ways, so step back and see if you always want the slack. Why should it always be you that gets a break?

Take time to look back at your relationship and see if you ignored your partner's needs at a time he needed an understanding or sympathetic moment. Maybe now what's happening is a little payback from your partner. What often happens is that a tit for tat or a tick tock mentality sets in. That is, I could cut you some slack, but I didn't get any from you when I needed it, so tough noogies. Don't do it. It is a sure way to possibly scar the relationship for good. Instead, stop, put your needs aside, and see what needs to be done to get you and your partner back to a safe, nurturing place—a place where both of you feel like talking without having to hear about the other's problems. There is no scorecard, and it's not always your turn. It is what it is, so take care of business.

You cannot offer too much kindness but you can sure deny it too much. Why is it that we remember the bad things our partner did to us but have to really think to recall the good things? Is it because we really did not get very many breaks or is it that we never give credit to the person when credit was earned?

If I may offer a suggestion, mentally write the bad things we think our partner does in pencil, and the good things in ink. By doing so, it is easier to erase the perceived bad things. After all, do you want someone to remember all your mistakes and bad behavior incidents? I don't think so. Address whatever the concern/complaint is at the time the transgression occurred, resolve it, erase it, forget it, and move on. Earlier in this book, I said to you, "When it's over, it's over." You can do it, so do it. I can tell you from my own relationships, as well as from my mediation cases, oftentimes, there is a miscommunication somewhere along the way. Go back, ask what was said, compare it to what you heard, and if it matches and you don't like it, I guess it's time to deal with it. If not, problem solved, you heard it wrong.

Time spent in discord is time wasted. It will never be recovered. What do you have to show for it except bad memories and scars on the relationship? When I say cut him some slack, I am not saying to acquiesce. What I am saying is to disagree if it's important in the big scheme. If not, give yourself and your partner a break. You will be surprised how good you will feel it you don't consistently find fault with your partner. If this has been the relationship pattern, it will take time for you to stop; it will take time for your partner to stop as well. Over time, a dysfunctional pattern sometimes develops where someone wants to be first to find fault in the other. In some way, he feels superior. Why not adopt the attitude to look for the good? In time maybe he will find you aren't so bad either. I have never met a couple that started dating or became married who didn't like each other in the beginning. Discord is insidious. It creeps into a relationship like a cancer, small at first, and then before we know it, we are consumed.

Whether you are young or not so young, remember to remain child-like, not childish. Children get into disagreements all the time, but they get over it. They stay friends and soon forget what they were fussing about. I do not know when we develop a sense of holding a grudge; bad plan. Adults, when they are childish, tend to want their way, hold a grudge and at least superficially, act like they don't care if the relationship goes in the ditch. Child-like behavior gives you both the opportunity to laugh at yourselves, each other and your childish ways.

Some really funny times can be had when we look back on our behavior and see it for what it was.

Notes, Questions and Conclusions
This is not a test, you cannot fail, so be honest with yourself.

_____

_____

_____

_____

_____

_____

_____

_____

_____

_____

_____

_____

_____

_____

_____

_____

_____

_____

_____

_____

_____

_____

Chapter 16

Conclusion

Well, now you have it; relationships made easy. Relationships, even good ones, are not difficult if you have the right partner and utilize the right relationship tools. The purpose of this book is multi-faceted, to give you some of those tools as well as these axioms:

1. The desire to never give up hope;

2. A map to keep you on the right road;

3. Confidence to stay in the hunt for "Right" not simply Mr./Mrs. "Right Now";

4. Knowledge that someone is looking for a fulfilling relationship, and if you both subscribe to the tenets discussed in this book, it will be you;

5. The unfortunate knowledge that you or your partner may have to choose to leave the relationship (remember, you may

be the one not compatible, so don't be throwing any rocks). It is possible that you can both see each other with a new perspective, so don't start packing just yet. Remember, you liked each other once upon a time. Now is a good time for forgiving and forgetting, on both sides. New ideas and new relationship tools; why not give each other an opportunity and build on the good times you have shared.

My sincere hope is that you can find or improve the many joys in your life. It does not matter if you are young or not as young as you used to be. You may be the person who likes to go at life alone; if so, go for it and quit worrying. The biblical Paul writes that some people are not meant to be married, so who are you to argue? If you want a partner, you should know after reading this book, that someone wants you as well. Life is full of uncertainty, so why not increase your odds for happiness and team up with a partner that has your best interest as well as their own in mind? There is nothing wrong with each of you feeling that you got the best deal. Together, you can improve the areas of compatibility using the methods discussed in this book.

When making one of our most important decisions, i.e., the person with whom you want to spend the rest of your life with, ask yourself "How much is my life worth?" Promise yourself to only accept what you deserve. The value of your life in God's calculation: He gave his only son for you.

I believe what I have written in this book is true and will be of benefit to anyone who follows the tenets. Hopefully it is so well written and the results are as expected, I will not be able to write a sequel. The only way I know how to improve the information presented in this book is to have its readers share with me how it has helped them in their quest for personal and partnership happiness.

If I have helped anyone find or increase his happiness, whether it is in himself or his relationship, I will consider this book and this life effort a success; consequently, I encourage you to share those discoveries with me.

I wish you all the best that life has to offer. Sometimes, life events seem to favor some over others; no one said life was fair, but if you're happy, who cares? For me, I know from painful personal experiences that life is horribly unfair, but I have a great wife, wonderful children, grandchildren and in-laws; the friends that I have are few but would do anything for me that I asked, and for that too, I am thankful.

So in closing, I would like to leave you with this thought:

I wrote this book for you, but in writing it, found that it was for me as well. I hope it can help all who have read it and with those with whom you share the tenets contained within.

Notes, Questions and Conclusions

This is not a test, you cannot fail, so be honest with yourself.

_____

_____

_____

_____

_____

_____

_____

_____

_____

_____

_____

_____

_____

_____

_____

_____

_____

_____

_____

_____

_____

_____

Chapter 17

What Comes After Conclusion?

Random Thoughts of Consciousness

Often times the portion of our brain that is in charge of our unconscious thoughts provides amazing clarity to a subject that was previously unclear. The following list is examples of some of those random thoughts that come seemingly from nowhere yet have significant impact in the way we process events in our everyday lives. I suggest you allow those thoughts to come forward, everyone has them, and some of us refuse to listen, even to ourselves.

o   He who loves the least controls the relationship.

o   Good sex cannot save a bad marriage, but bad sex can ruin a good one.

o   Give 100% to your partner, you will never be sorry.

o   Marriage is the most important partnership ever created. Work on it as hard as you do your day job.

o   Don't quit your night job.

o   The honeymoon does not have to be over.

o   Don't go to bed angry, even if it takes all night to resolve the conflict.

o   Remember, since this is the person with whom you want to be happy for the rest of your life, why waste time together in anger and discord?

o   Relationships should not be costly in terms of emotional, physical or spiritual expense.

o   Stay focused on the facts; leave opinions and emotions out of any misunderstanding. Don't give up or give in, find out where the train left the track and the wreck ensued. Let the person responsible be accountable.

o   Defend yourself when necessary but only from a position of love, not fear or anger.

o Symptoms do not grow into problems, but problems do create symptoms.

o Learn to trust your mistrust.

o No one is perfect, and that includes you.

o Think with your brain; feel with your heart; make decisions accordingly.

o Almost anyone regardless of gender, especially those spiritually and morally conflicted, is susceptible to wandering outside the relationship boundaries. Intellectually you may know it is wrong, but you do it anyway. It is not always about sex, in fact, rarely is it.

o Sex is composed of three parts: preparation, execution and recovery. They are all important, so don't skip any.

o Don't both be mad at the same time.

o Feelings...Feelings come from our thoughts. Our thoughts come from what we tell ourselves. What are you telling yourself?

o   Because you feel someway does not make it true, i.e., I feel stupid, I feel fat. Match your feelings with facts. If they don't match, change what you tell yourself. If they do match, stop being critical of yourself; tell yourself something positive each day.

o   For every high there is a corresponding low of equal depth and duration as was the height and duration of the high.

o   No animals were harmed or killed during the writing of this book. (What? You thought I would let you leave on a somber note? Go out and make your life like you want it to be.)

Notes, Questions and Conclusions

This is not a test, you cannot fail, so be honest with yourself.

_____

_____

_____

_____

_____

_____

_____

_____

_____

_____

_____

_____

_____

_____

_____

_____

_____

_____

_____

_____

_____

_____

_____

Testimonial

"We found the book entertaining as well as thought-provoking. We can see it being a great tool for group discussions. There are many valuable insights: eliminating the "blame" game; the discussion of the "C's" and the need to examine (and own) your needs and responses; deciding what you *really* want in relationships; the absolute importance of honesty and trust. We appreciated the Biblical applications and the unapologetic foundation of Ronnie's observations being grounded in his own spiritual beliefs.

What we really found encouraging was that our relationship is based on the solid principals stated in Ronnie's book. We have the Chemistry and Consistency, and all of the Compatibilities that he discussed. Even the "leaving the commode lid up" issue was something we addressed early on, agreed upon, and then let go. We discovered we could talk with and listen to each other during our long telephone conversations, and that skill has been valuable as we've learned to live with each other. Ronnie's book seems to promote the plan of learning to communicate well from the beginning...with nothing hidden...and we've proven that to be a very successful model to follow.

In short, we would recommend this book as a study for anyone wanting a healthy relationship. Singles looking, happy couples, and couples in difficulty would all benefit from his insight and guidance.

We do hope he begins teaching this material by facilitating some groups. That experience would give him even greater insight and tweak some of the existing material."

Ray and Ann Buck
Focused On Him Ministries

Made in the USA
Columbia, SC
05 May 2018